EARTH'S TREASURES

GOLD

CHRISTINE PETERSEN
ABDO Publishing Company

visit us at
www.abdopublishing.com

Published by ABDO Publishing Company, PO Box 398166, Minneapolis, MN 55439.
Copyright © 2014 by Abdo Consulting Group, Inc. International copyrights reserved in all
countries. No part of this book may be reproduced in any form without written permission from the
publisher. The Checkerboard Library™ is a trademark and logo of ABDO Publishing Company.

Printed in the United States of America, North Mankato, Minnesota.
052013
012014

 PRINTED ON RECYCLED PAPER

Cover Photo: iStockphoto
Interior Photos: Alamy pp. 23, 24; AP Images pp. 5, 15, 18; Corbis p. 4; Getty Images pp. 10, 11, 17,
    21, 25; Glow Images p. 9; iStockphoto pp. 1, 26–27; Library of Congress p. 19;
    NASA/MSFC/David Higginbotham p. 13; Science Source pp. 6–7, 15, 16;
    Thinkstock pp. 8, 28, 29

Editors: Rochelle Baltzer, Megan M. Gunderson
Art Direction: Neil Klinepier

Library of Congress Control Number: 2013932670

Cataloging-in-Publication Data

Petersen, Christine.
 Gold / Christine Petersen.
  p. cm. -- (Earth's treasures)
ISBN 978-1-61783-871-2
Includes bibliographical references and index.
1. Gold--Juvenile literature. 2. Precious metals--Juvenile literature.   I. Title.
669/.22--dc23

                                                                    2013932670

CONTENTS

ANCIENT TREASURE

On January 4, 1928, **archaeologist** Leonard Woolley prepared a telegram. He had exciting news to share with his coworkers at the University of Pennsylvania. In fact, it was so exciting that he wrote the message in Latin to help keep his secret safe!

For five years, Woolley and his team had worked in the desert of what is now southern Iraq. They were slowly digging up an ancient city called Ur. Now they had found a special tomb. Inside it lay the body of Puabi, queen of Ur.

In Queen Puabi's tomb, Woolley found gold cups.

Leonard Woolley at Ur. He became Sir Leonard Woolley when he was knighted in 1935.

The queen even had a drinking straw made of gold! Attendants surrounded her. Guards with copper daggers protected the entrance.

Queen Puabi's head was wrapped in more than 24 feet (7.3 m) of gold ribbon. She had a gold comb and earrings. And she had an elaborate gold headdress with wreaths of golden leaves. She wore a cloak made of 86 strands of more than 1,600 gold, lapis lazuli, and carnelian beads.

The queen had lain in her tomb for more than 4,000 years. Yet her treasure shone as brightly as the day she had died.

Queen Puabi's golden headdress

ELEMENTAL

What is gold? It is a chemical element. Elements are the natural ingredients that form everything on our planet.

There are more than 100 different elements. Nitrogen is the most abundant element in Earth's atmosphere. Your body contains large amounts of nitrogen, carbon, hydrogen, and oxygen.

An element is made of just one kind of atom. Atoms can mix and match to form compounds called molecules. Inside the earth, atoms are the building blocks of minerals. They bond in repeating patterns to form three-dimensional crystals.

Most minerals are built from at least two chemical elements. Gold is different. It contains only atoms of gold. These pack together tightly to form crystals.

Gold crystals are usually too small to see. They sometimes grow in groups that look like flakes or grains. More rarely, gold forms larger nuggets or clumps.

The chemical symbol for gold is Au. This comes from the Latin word aurum, *which means "shining dawn."*

GOOD AS GOLD

Nearly 80 percent of elements, including gold, are metals. Metals share certain important and useful qualities. They are generally solid at room temperature. They are shiny. Metals are **malleable** and **ductile**. Electricity and heat flow easily through objects made of metal.

People may have first noticed gold in nature because of its **luster**. Light reflects brightly off its surface. Gold is also the most malleable metal. A small piece can be hammered to form a sheet far thinner than notebook paper.

In addition, gold is the most ductile metal. It may be cut, twisted, or pulled into different shapes. Royalty once wore clothing woven with slender gold threads.

Thin gold wires and connectors are found

An ounce of gold, which is about the weight of a quarter, could create a sheet of gold stretching 100 square feet (9.3 sq m)!

inside modern electronics like phones and computers. Just one troy ounce (31 g) of gold can become a wire 50 miles (80 km) long!

You have probably seen metal objects that look dull or stained. Copper roof tiles develop a green film called patina. Iron objects become orange with rust in damp air. So how did Queen Puabi's treasure remain so beautiful after thousands of years? Gold does not **corrode**, rust, or tarnish!

Gold leaf is extremely thin! It can take more than 7,000 layers just to equal the thickness of a dime!

The Goldsmith's Art

Gold has always been used to make beautiful objects. Books were written by hand in **medieval** Europe. Fancy letters and borders were added to the pages using powdered gold or gold leaf. Gilt is a thin layer of gold attached to the surface of picture frames and other objects. Gold jewelry and decorations can be engraved by carving or cutting designs onto their surfaces.

Today, about 60 percent of jewelry is manufactured using lost-wax casting. **Goldsmiths** in Egypt invented this method 4,000 years ago! Over time, the process was lost and rediscovered several times around the world.

In lost-wax casting, a goldsmith designs a shape or pattern using wax. The wax is covered in plaster of Paris or layers of clay.

Once hardened, this is fired in a **kiln**. The wax melts, or is "lost." A hollow, detailed mold remains. The goldsmith pours melted gold inside. When everything cools, the mold is broken to remove the gold object.

Gold items made using the lost-wax casting process

METAL OF MANY USES

The properties of gold make it useful as well as beautiful. Recall that gold is used in electronic devices. This is a good choice because electricity flows easily through gold. Dentists sometimes make gold fillings. Because gold does not **corrode**, these provide a long-lasting fix.

Heat from the Sun can damage satellites in space. Gold reflects as much as 98 percent of the Sun's harmful rays. It doesn't take much gold to do the job. On a space helmet, a layer of gold thin enough to see through protects astronauts.

Scientists at **NASA** are using gold on a new space telescope. Its mirrors are coated with a layer of gold one-thousandth the thickness of a human hair! The Webb Telescope will collect pictures of deep space. This will help scientists learn about the earliest galaxies.

Gold has always been valuable because it is rare. It has been used to make coins for almost 3,000 years. Today, the US government keeps a reserve of gold bars at Fort Knox in Kentucky. Each bar is about the size of an ordinary brick. It weighs 27.5 pounds (12.5 kg)!

It takes just 0.1 ounces (3 g) of gold to cover a mirror on the Webb measuring four feet (1.2 m) across.

LODE GOLD

If you took a sample from almost any rock on Earth, there would probably be gold in it. Seawater also contains gold. In fact, there is an estimated 15,000 tons (13,600 t) of gold in the world's oceans.

Here's the bad news. Most of this gold is too scarcely distributed to be gathered. It would be very slow and expensive to collect. Gold worth collecting is found in lode or placer deposits.

So how does gold form deposits? Scientists have several ideas. One starts with **magma** entering Earth's crust. It heats water in the crust. This water **dissolves** surrounding rock, which contains atoms of metals such as gold. When the water cools, the gold separates out and forms veins. These deposits can later be mined.

Another idea says that gold may come from magma itself. When magma cools, gold solutions separate out and form **ores**. A third theory has to do with metamorphic rock. As the rock forms, minerals rearrange and water is released. This water carries gold from the original rock. It moves toward Earth's surface, cools, and forms gold deposits.

In these vein, or lode, deposits gold is often found with another mineral called quartz. Gold may be found in its native form. Or, it may be mixed with silver or other elements. Gold **ores** are found near the surface and deep underground.

The quartz in this rock may indicate gold is nearby.

Gold leaf magnified 1.5 million times

Placer Gold

Lode deposits formed deep underground millions of years ago. But Earth is constantly changing. The planet's rocky surface is like a giant jigsaw puzzle. It is made up of several large pieces called plates.

The plates float side by side atop the hot, molten mantle. Over time, they slowly move. Plate movements produce earthquakes and volcanoes. New rocks may be formed and old rocks may change.

At Earth's surface, rocks are lashed by sand, wind, and rain. Small pieces chip off. The rock becomes pitted and rough. These spaces fill with water. When the water

Don't Get Fooled!

Pyrite is sometimes mistaken for gold. You might know this mineral better as fool's gold! It is made of the elements iron and sulfur instead of gold. Pyrite is also harder and lighter than real gold.

Placer is pronounced "PLA-suhr."

freezes in winter, it expands. This causes the rock to crack and break down even more. Entire mountains slowly crumble by this slow, steady process of erosion. Minerals and metals trapped within the rock are released.

Because gold is so **dense**, pieces of the shiny metal wash downhill. They settle with other pebbles in riverbeds. In this way, the gold forms placer deposits.

IN A RUSH!

In 1848, James Marshall was building a water-powered sawmill in California for John Sutter. Workers dug a long trench to carry water from the American River through the sawmill.

On the morning of January 24, Marshall went out to check the trench. A flash of light in the water caught his eye. Marshall reached into the water and found bits of gold!

Marshall had found placer gold. The news spread faster than wildfire. California was quickly flooded with people hoping to strike it rich.

James Marshall

The California gold rush lasted for decades. Similar gold rushes happened in other parts of North America and in Australia and South Africa. Ninety percent of all the gold ever mined has been collected since the California gold rush!

Thousands of prospectors arrived to seek their fortunes as gold was discovered throughout the western United States.

You're the Miner

You can see what it was like to be a miner during the California gold rush. Visit Marshall Gold Discovery State Historic Park in California. It marks the spot where James Marshall found gold. Or, find adventure in Alaska. Gold panning is allowed at Petersville Recreational Mining Area.

To pan for gold, stake out a spot beside a river or stream. Scoop a pile of river gravel into a wide, flat pan. Swirl the pan slowly in the water. Sand and other light materials will float over the top. Gold will settle to the bottom of the pan.

Become a Rock Hound!

WOULD YOU LIKE TO START YOUR OWN COLLECTION OF GEMS AND MINERALS? BECOME A ROCK HOUND!

To get started, locate a site likely to have the treasures you seek. Before you head out, be sure it is legal and you have permission to collect specimens from your search area. Then, gather the tools and safety gear you'll need. Don't forget to bring an adult!

Label your treasures with the date and location you found them. Many rock hounds set a goal for their collections. For example, they might gather samples of all the minerals found in their state or province.

Finally, always leave the land in better shape than you found it. Respecting the environment helps preserve it for future rock hounds and the rest of your community.

WHAT WILL YOU NEED?

map
compass
magnifying glass
hard hat or bicycle helmet
safety goggles
sunscreen
bucket
shovel
rock hammer
pan or screen box
containers for your finds

You will probably find only tiny flakes or grains of gold. These are still very beautiful! Bring a magnifying glass and tweezers to examine your treasures. Display your finds and tell your friends how they were collected. Gold makes an impressive start to a mineral or rock collection.

Gold panning isn't complicated, but it requires a lot of patience!

Digging Deep

Gold is mined around the world, including at sites in the United States and Canada. Other important sources of gold are South Africa, Russia, and Australia. At the end of the 1900s, they provided two-thirds of the world's gold production!

Modern gold mining requires heavy equipment and special technology. In surface mines, the ground is blasted with explosives so that **ore** can be removed. The rock is cut away in layers, each deeper than the last. These layers look like the steps of a stadium.

Gold can also be removed from lode deposits far below the surface. The world's deepest mine is in South Africa. It descends 2.5 miles (4 km)! Miners ride to work each day in elevators that travel 40 miles per hour (65 kph).

Deep in the mine, fans are used to cool the miners and provide fresh air as they work. At such depths, the rock reaches temperatures of up to 140 degrees Fahrenheit (60°C).

At Australia's Super Pit, mining takes place 24 hours a day, 365 days a year. It is the nation's largest open-pit gold mine.

Gold must be separated from other substances in an **ore**. This step requires chemicals, heat, or electricity. The amount of gold in any rock is very small. Place two quarters on your palm. Together they weigh about 0.4 ounces (11 g). The best mines produce only about this much gold from every 10 tons (9 t) of ore.

Black Hills gold is famous for its range of colors.

When sold, the purity of gold is listed in karats. Pure gold is 24 karats. It is extremely rare and valuable. Pure gold is also quite soft. So, jewelers prefer to work with alloys.

Alloys are mixtures of gold with other metals such as silver, copper, zinc, nickel, or platinum. Making an alloy adds strength to gold and can change its color in appealing ways. Pure gold is sun yellow. Mixed with other metals, gold can be silver-white, green, orange-red, or even pink!

All the gold ever refined would barely fill two Olympic-sized pools! And more than half of that has happened in just the last 50 years.

North
America

South
America

Top Gold-
Producing Countries

Australia   Mexico
Canada   Peru
China   Russia
Ghana   South Africa
Indonesia   United States

GOLD'S FUTURE

For hundreds of years, people looked for ways to make gold. They believed in a process called transmutation. If it worked, an atom of one element could be changed into another.

The recipe for gold required a common metal like lead to be mixed with the legendary **Philosopher's Stone**. Over the centuries, many people tried to make this precious metal. None of them ever figured it out.

Today, scientists really can make gold. Atoms of lead are placed into a machine called a particle accelerator. Lead has more **protons** than gold. The particle accelerator makes three protons break free from a lead atom. The result is gold! This is a fascinating discovery. But it is still far less expensive to mine gold from the ground.

Each year, two-thirds of the gold used commercially is used for jewelry.

Confusing Karats

Karat is a measure of the purity of gold. Carat describes the weight of gemstones. A carrot is something you eat!

Gold is a precious and limited resource. Recycling is an important way to preserve our supply. Gold can be collected from old electronics, dental fillings, and jewelry. It is melted down and used again. If we make careful choices, gold will always be available to light our lives.

Gold atoms are one in a billion! For every 1 billion atoms in Earth's crust, just one is gold.

29

GLOSSARY

archaeologist (ahr-kee-AH-luh-jihst) - one who studies the remains of people and activities from ancient times.

corrode - to wear away gradually by chemical action.

dense - having a high mass per unit volume.

dissolve - to cause to pass into solution or become liquid.

ductile - able to be bent or pulled into different shapes.

goldsmith - a smith is an artisan who makes things out of metal. Goldsmiths work with gold.

kiln - an oven, a furnace, or a heated area. It is used to process a substance by burning, firing, or drying.

luster - a shiny quality, especially from reflected light.

magma - melted rock beneath Earth's surface.

malleable - able to be stretched or shaped by the beating of a hammer.

medieval - of or belonging to the Middle Ages. The Middle Ages was a period in European history from about 500 to 1500.

NASA - National Aeronautics and Space Administration. NASA is a US government agency that manages the nation's space program and conducts flight research.

ore - a mineral deposit containing something such as metal that is valuable enough to be mined.

Philosopher's Stone - a stone, substance, or chemical believed to be able to turn other metals into gold.

proton - a very small particle that has a positive charge. It is part of the nucleus of an atom.

SAYING IT

karat - KEHR-uht
metamorphic - meh-tuh-MAWR-fihk

WEB SITES

To learn more about gold, visit ABDO Publishing Company online. Web sites about gold are featured on our Book Links page. These links are routinely monitored and updated to provide the most current information available.

www.abdopublishing.com

INDEX